How did Gooseberry Patch get started?

You may know the story of Gooseberry Patch ... the tale of two country friends who decided one day over the backyard fence to try their hands at the mail order business. Started in Jo Ann's kitchen back in 1984, Vickie & Jo Ann's dream of "A Country Store in Your Mailbox®" has grown and grown to a 96-page catalog with over 400 products, including cookie cutters, Santas, snowmen, gift baskets, angels and our very own line of cookbooks! What an adventure for two country friends!

The Country Friends Collection® just naturally came about, since Vickie & Jo Ann are very much like Kate, Holly & Mary Elizabeth ... each has her own way of doing things. (Jo Ann drinks coffee; Vickie drinks tea ... Jo Ann likes chocolate with crunchy nuts; Vickie likes the creamy centers ... Jo Ann manages the business end; Vickie directs the creative.) You'll find Vickie & Jo Ann's personalities in everything we offer, and we hope you enjoy our "Country Friends" as much as we do!

Your friends at Gooseberry Patch

★ If you like this edition of THE COUNTRY FRIENDS COLLECTION®, you'll love our Gooseberry Patch catalog!

For a two-year subscription to "A COUNTRY STORE IN YOUR MAILBOX"® filled with cookbooks, cookie cutters, snowmen, angels, Santas, & hundreds of other country collectibles, send $3.00 to:

Gooseberry Patch
PO Box 190 ~ DEPT. Leaflets
DELAWARE, OHIO 43015
PHONE 1-800/854-6673 FAX 1-740/363-7225

Cozy Fall Picnic

BLANKET IN A BACKPACK instructions on page 12

SCARF and **REVERSIBLE HAT** instructions on pages 12-13

MITTENS

Basics, page 18; Pattern, page 19

- 1/4 yd red fleece
- 8 decorative buttons
- embroidery floss
- tracing paper

Adjust pattern size as needed. Match right sides and use a 1/2" seam allowance for all sewing unless otherwise noted. Trim seam allowances close to stitching.

For each mitten, cut 2 mitten shapes from red fleece. Leaving wrist open, sew mitten shapes together. Turn mitten right side out. Pin opening edge 1/4" to inside; blanket stitch around opening to secure. Sew buttons to back of mitten.

FOCUS ON **PEOPLE** INSTEAD OF ACTIVITIES & OBJECTS. SPEND SOME QUIET TIME WITH YOUR **FAMILY.**

Snuggle Up at Home

MONOGRAM THROW

Basics, page 18; Pattern, page 23

- 1 1/2 yds red fleece
- 1 1/3 yds green fleece
- embroidery floss
- rotary cutter and cutting mat

Cut one 46"x56" piece each from red and green fleece. Enlarge desired letter 320% on a photocopier. Cut out monogram from red fleece. Center and pin monogram on right side of green fleece 7" from one short edge. Use 3 strands of floss to blanket stitch letter to green fleece. Matching wrong sides and using 6 strands of floss, blanket stitch long edges of red and green fleece together. Cutting through both layers of fleece, cut 1/2"x3" fringe strips along short edges. Tie each top and bottom fringe strip together with a single wrap.

♥I know not why, but home is dearest.♥ CICERO 106 - 43 B.C.

Pretty Pillows to Give

MONOGRAM PILLOW

Basics, page 18; Pattern, page 23

- 1/2 yd red fleece
- 1/2 yd green fleece
- embroidery floss
- 12"x16" pillow form
- rotary cutter and cutting mat

Cut one 13"x20" piece each from red and green fleece. Enlarge desired letter 320% on a photocopier. Cut out monogram from red fleece. For pillow top, center and pin monogram on right side of green fleece. Blanket stitch letter to pillow top. Matching right sides, use a 1/2" seam allowance to sew long edges of pillow top and bottom together; turn right side out. Cut 1/2"x2" fringe strips along short edges of pillow through top and bottom layers of fleece. Insert pillow form. Tie each top and bottom fringe strip together with a single wrap.

NINE-PATCH PILLOW instructions on page 13

Oh-So Comfy

JACKET

Basics, page 18; Pattern, page 21

- $1^3/_8$ yds rose fleece
- $^5/_8$ yd mustard fleece
- embroidery floss
- tracing paper
- fabric marking pen

Felt and Fleece Flowers

Basics, page 18; Patterns, page 21

- rose felt
- scrap of dark green fleece
- two $^5/_8$" dia. brown shank-style buttons

Our jacket is a women's size small/medium; adjust the amount of fleece and pattern size as needed. Match right sides and raw edges and use a $^1/_2$" seam allowance for all sewing unless otherwise noted.

For jacket, cut a 41"x53" piece from rose fleece. Matching short ends, fold in half. Pin neck pattern at center of fold; mark cutting lines. Referring to Cutting Diagram, page 14, mark remaining cutting lines. Cut along lines marked in blue on diagram through both thicknesses. Cut along red lines through jacket front only.

continued on page 14

A well ★ spent day brings happy sleep.
-Leonardo da Vinci-

NECK WARMER

Basics, page 18
- 1/2 yd plaid fabric
- 5/8 yd mustard fleece
- two 3/4"x5" hook and loop fastener strips
- embroidery floss
- 4 lbs uncooked rice
- tracing paper

Felt and Fleece Flower
Basics, page 18; Patterns, page 21
- rose felt
- scrap of dark green fleece
- 5/8" dia. brown shank-style button

SLIPPERS instructions on page 15

Place your rice bag in the microwave for 3 minutes to heat or in the freezer till chilled. Match right sides and raw edges and use a 1/2" seam allowance for all sewing unless otherwise noted.

For rice bag, cut two 8"x25" pieces from plaid fabric. Center and sew the soft side of each hook and loop strip 1 1/2" in from ends on right side of one fabric piece. Press one end of each fabric piece 1/2" to wrong side. Leaving pressed end open for turning, sew pieces together; turn right side out. Measuring from sewn end of bag, mark across bag at 6" intervals. Pour 1 3/4 cups of rice into bag; sew along drawn line. Repeat to fill each section; sew opening closed.

For cover, cut two 8"x 26" pieces from mustard fleece. Using the strips on the rice bag for placement guides, sew the rough side of each hook and loop strip to short ends on wrong side of one fleece piece. Sew together along ends and one long edge; turn right side out. For ties, cut ten 1"x10" strips from mustard fleece lengthwise (not selvage to selvage). Pinning 1" of each strip to inside of cover, evenly space 5 strips on each side of cover; sew strips in place. Blanket stitch along sewn edges and around top edge. Sew Felt and Fleece Flower to front of cover.

Just for Baby

BABY BLANKET

Basics, page 18; Patterns, pages 25-27

- $1^1/_3$ yds blue textured fleece for blanket front
- $1^1/_3$ yds yellow textured fleece for blanket back and sun
- $^1/_2$ yd white fleece
- $3^3/_4$ yds of $^3/_8$" wide yellow grosgrain ribbon
- tracing paper
- embroidery floss
- polyester fiberfill
- rotary cutter and cutting mat

Use 6 strands of floss to work running stitches and 3 strands for blanket stitches.

Enlarge big cloud pattern 126% on photocopier. Cut a 44" square each from blue and yellow fleece. Cut sun from yellow fleece. Cut a circle $^1/_4$" smaller than sun pattern, 2 small clouds and 2 enlarged big clouds from white fleece. Cut one big cloud along dotted lines. Referring to Placement Diagram, page 16, for lengths, cut ribbon for sun rays.

continued on page 16

BABY BOY JACKET AND CAP instructions on page 17

BABY GIRL JACKET AND CAP

Basics, page 18;
Patterns, pages 28-29

- 5/8 yd yellow textured fleece
- 1/4 yd white fleece
- 2 ribbon rosettes
- sewing snap
- embroidery floss

Match right sides and raw edges and use a 1/4" seam allowance for all sewing unless otherwise noted. When cutting out pieces, make sure fleece stretches across pieces horizontally. Our finished cap has a 16" head opening; adjust the size of fleece rectangles as needed.

Enlarge jacket and cuff patterns 135% on photocopier. For jacket, use enlarged pattern to cut one jacket back and 2 (one in reverse) jacket fronts from yellow fleece. Cut along red line on jacket fronts only. Cut one collar and 4 enlarged cuffs from white fleece. Sew one cuff to end of each sleeve. Sew jacket fronts to jacket back along shoulder seams. Sew side seams from bottom of jacket to end of cuffs; clip seams under arms. Matching top center of back of jacket and center of straight edge of collar, pin right side of collar to wrong side of jacket as shown (**Fig. 1**, page 16). Sew collar to jacket; clip seams. Turn jacket right side out. Fold cuffs into sleeves along seam; blindstitch raw edges of cuffs in sleeves.

continued on page 16

LAMB

Basics, page 18; Patterns, page 31

- $^1/_4$ yd fuzzy white fur fleece
- scraps of ecru, tan and black felt
- $^1/_2$ yd of $^5/_8$" wide yellow striped satin ribbon
- $^1/_2$ cup uncooked rice
- polyester fiberfill

Match right sides and raw edges and use a $^1/_4$" seam allowance for all sewing unless otherwise noted.

Enlarge patterns 117% on photocopier. Cut 2 body pieces, 2 ears and a tail from fleece. Cut a face, a tail, 2 ears and 4 feet from ecru felt. Cut 2 eyes from black felt and a nose from tan felt. Leaving straight edge open, sew a felt ear to each fleece ear; turn right side out. Repeat for tail.

continued on page 17

What a difference it makes to come home to a Child! —Margaret Fuller

A baby is such a nice way to start a person.

The heart has
its own memory
like the mind,
and in it are enshrined
the precious keepsakes,
into which is wrought
the giver's loving thought.
- Longfellow -

BOO-BOO BUDDY

Basics, page 18; Patterns, pages 29-30

- 1/4 yd fuzzy ecru fleece
- two 5" squares of light yellow fleece
- 3/4 yd jumbo yellow chenille rickrack
- scraps of blue and pink felt
- embroidery floss
- tissue paper
- fabric glue
- 1 1/2 cups uncooked rice

Keep your boo-boo buddy chilled in the freezer.

Cut 2 faces from yellow fleece, 2 squares from fuzzy fleece, teardrop from blue felt and 2 cheeks from pink felt. Glue felt shapes to faces. Work French knots for eyes and running stitches for mouths. Blanket stitch each face to center of one fleece square. Matching wrong sides and tucking rickrack between layers, pin squares together. Leaving an opening for filling, zigzag stitch pieces together along edges of square. Fill boo-boo buddy with rice and zigzag stitch closed.

BLANKET IN A BACKPACK

Photo, page 2; Basics, page 18

- 40"x60" plaid fleece rectangle for blanket
- two 18" plaid fleece squares for backpack
- 3"x14" plaid fleece strip, cut lengthwise (not selvage to selvage)
- two 42" lengths of 1" wide black nylon webbing for drawstring
- two 28" lengths of 1½" wide black cotton webbing for straps (Adjust length as needed.)

Match right sides and use a ½" seam allowance for all sewing unless otherwise noted. Hold a lit match to each end of nylon webbing to keep nylon from fraying.

For handle, fold long edges of 3"x14" strip to the center. Fold along center and topstitch along long edges.

For drawstring casings, fold top edge of each square 2" to wrong side; sew along long raw edges. Folding one end of each strap under 2", center and pin straps on right side of one square just below casing; stitch as shown (**Fig. 1**). Pin opposite ends of straps along bottom edge of square, 1" in from corners. Pin handle to wrong side of square.

Fig. 1

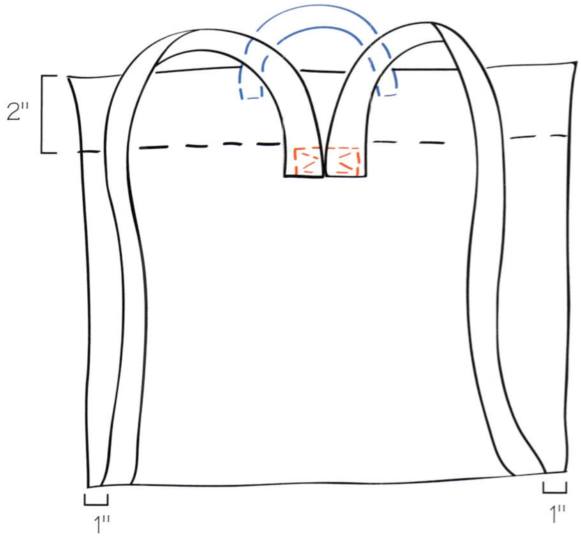

With strap side up and casing at top, pin square with straps to corner of blanket. Topstitch along top edge of square. Matching raw edges, pin remaining square, wrong side up, on square with straps. Beginning and ending at casing seam, sew squares to blanket along sides and bottom edges.

For drawstrings, beginning and ending on one side of backpack, use a large safety pin to thread one drawstring through both casings; knot ends together. Repeat with remaining drawstring, beginning and ending on opposite side of casing. Turn backpack right side out and tuck blanket inside backpack to carry.

SCARF

Photo, page 3; Basics, page 18

- 5"x48" red fleece strip
- 5"x56" plaid fleece strip
- 8 assorted buttons
- embroidery floss
- rotary cutter and cutting mat

Center red strip on plaid strip. Blanket stitch along long edges to join strips. Cut fringe along ends of plaid strip. Sew buttons along ends of red strip.

REVERSIBLE HAT

Photo, page 3; Basics, page 18; Pattern, page 20

- 1/3 yd red fleece
- 1/3 yd plaid fleece
- embroidery floss
- tracing paper

Our finished hat has a 21 3/4" head opening; adjust the pattern size as needed. Match right sides and use a 1/2" seam allowance for all sewing unless otherwise noted. Trim seam allowances close to stitching.

Enlarge hat shape 112% on photocopier. Cut 3 hat shapes each from red and plaid fleece. Sew red shapes together along curved edges. Sew plaid shapes together along curved edges. Matching right sides and seams and leaving an opening for turning, sew plaid and red hats together along bottom edge. Turn right side out; sew opening closed. Blanket stitch around bottom edge of hat. Turn cuff up 2".

NINE-PATCH PILLOW

Photo, page 5; Basics, page 18

- 1/2 yd red fleece
- 1/2 yd green fleece
- embroidery floss
- four 7/8" diameter buttons from covered button kits
- 4 red wooden beads with 1/2" dia. opening
- rotary cutter and cutting mat
- 14" square pillow form
- 2 1/2" square of cardboard

Cut three 5"x15" strips each from red and green fleece. Cut one 15" square from green fleece for pillow back. Matching long edges, lay green strips side by side. Weave red strips through green strips to make pillow front; pin to secure. Baste 1/4" around woven edge. Matching right sides and raw edges, pin pillow back to pillow front. Leaving one edge open for turning, use a 1/2" seam allowance to sew pieces together. Turn right side out and insert pillow form; sew opening closed. Cover buttons with red fleece and sew to pillow front.

For each tassel, cut two 1/4"x15" lengthwise (not selvage to selvage) strips each from red and green fleece. Tape a 12" length of floss at corners of top edge of cardboard piece. Beginning at bottom edge, refer to **Fig. 1** to carefully wrap each fleece strip around cardboard. Remove tape from floss and tie a tight knot around wrapped fleece. Slide fleece from cardboard; cut loops. Insert floss and top of tassel through bead. Sew tassel to corner of pillow.

Fig. 1

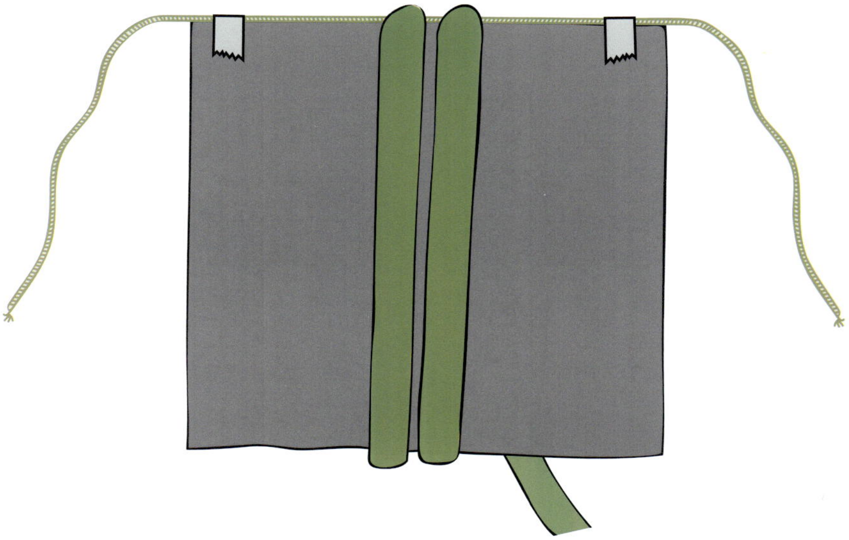

JACKET

continued from page 6

Cutting Diagram

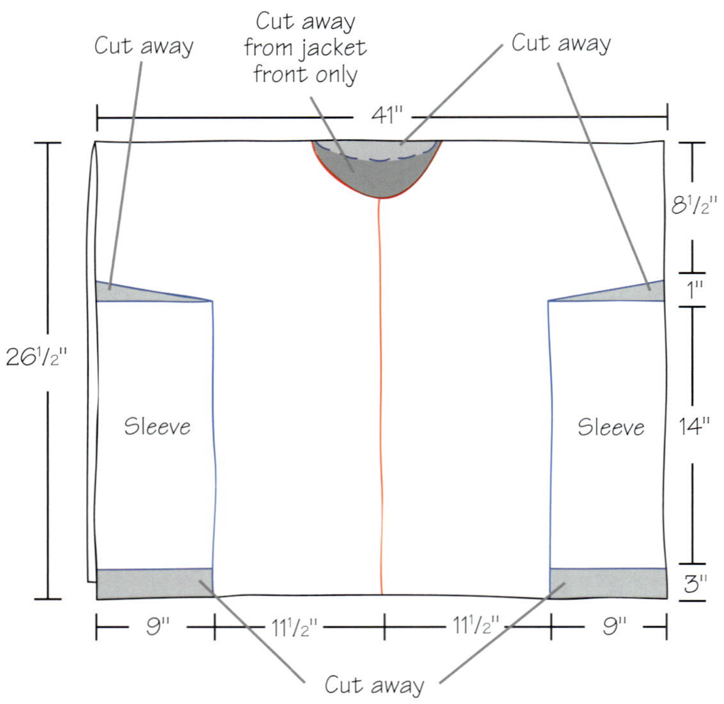

For neck and lapel facing on inside of jacket, refer to Facing Cutting Diagram to cut an 18"x36½" piece from mustard fleece; fold 10" of top end to back. Place neck pattern at center of folded edge; mark cutting lines. Cut along blue line of pattern through both thicknesses, then cut along red lines through front only; unfold facing. Cut along green lines to trim excess fabric.

Facing Cutting Diagram

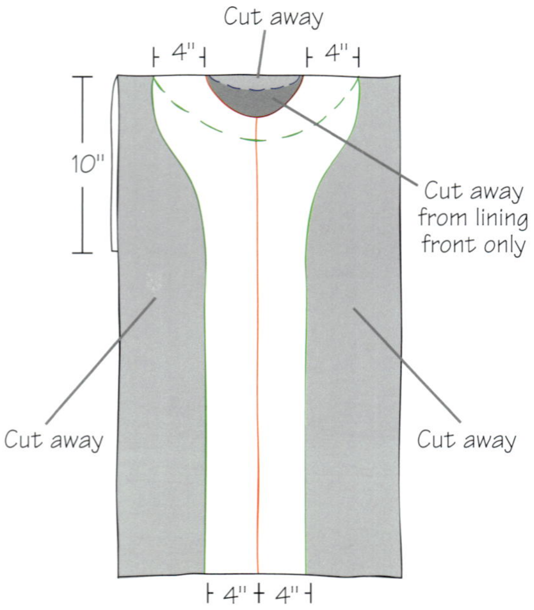

Sew facing to jacket front, bottom and neck opening; trim seam allowances to ¼". Clip corners and curves and turn facing to inside of jacket.

For each sleeve, sew 2 sleeve pieces together along one long side. Matching seam with shoulder of jacket, sew sleeve to jacket. For each cuff, cut one 6"x17" piece from mustard fleece. Sew cuff to wrist of sleeve.

Sew each side seam from bottom of jacket to end of cuff; trim seam allowances to ¼". Fold cuff inside sleeve; topstitch ½" from fold. Blindstitch raw edge of cuff to inside sleeve.

Fold bottom of jacket ½" to wrong side; topstitch ¼" from fold. Topstitch ½" from seam along jacket front and neck openings. Blindstitch raw edge of facing to inside jacket. Blanket stitch around bottom, front, neck and cuffs of jacket.

For each pocket, cut one 6"x6½" piece from rose fleece and one 2½"x6" piece from mustard fleece. Sew band to top of pocket along 6" side; turn right side out. Topstitch ¼" from seam, then blanket stitch along bottom edge of band. Pin pocket on jacket and topstitch ¼" from side and bottom edges. Blanket stitch along sides and bottom of pocket. Sew Felt and Fleece Flower to top of pocket.

SLIPPERS

Photo, page 7; Basics, page 18; Patterns, page 24

- 1/2 yd dark green fleece
- fusible interfacing
- tracing paper
- 1" thick foam
- embroidery floss

Felt and Fleece Flowers

Basics, page 18; Patterns, page 21

- rose felt
- scrap of mustard fleece
- two 5/8" dia. brown shank-style buttons

Our slippers fit most women's sizes; adjust the length of the pattern at heel as needed. Match right sides and raw edges and use a 1/2" seam allowance for all sewing unless otherwise noted.

Enlarge patterns 111% on photocopier. Cut two 2 1/4"x28" strips and 4 (2 in reverse) of each pattern piece from dark green fleece and from interfacing. Fuse interfacing to wrong side of all pieces. Take a stitch with a length of floss to mark dot where indicated on pattern pieces. Cut 2 foam pieces 1/2" smaller than bottom piece on all sides.

For each slipper, sew 2 toe pieces together along top edge; clip curves and turn right side out. Blanket stitch along sewn edge. Matching dots, sew wrong side of toe to right side of first bottom piece as shown (**Fig 1**). Remove floss marker.

Fig. 1

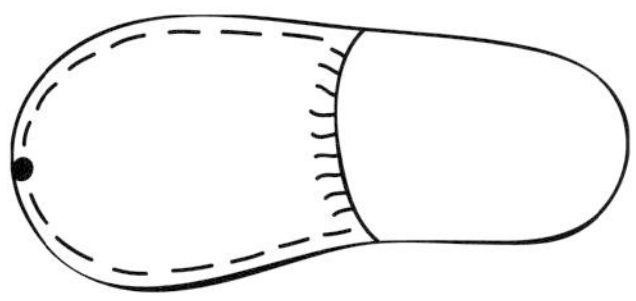

Fold one end of fleece strip 1/2" to wrong side. Beginning with folded end along inside arch of slipper and working toward the toe, pin fleece strip around first bottom piece as shown (**Fig. 2**), overlapping folded end by 1"; trim end.

Fig. 2

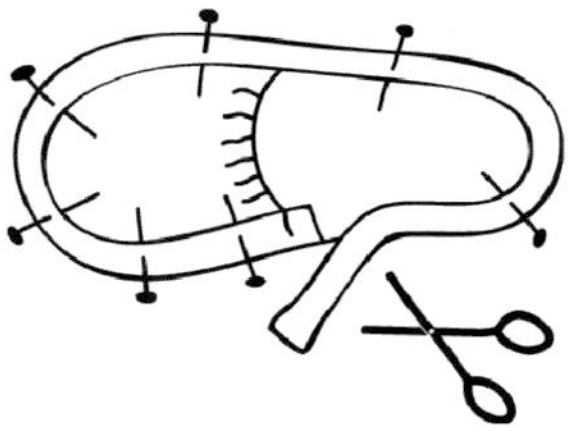

Sew in place. Leaving an opening for inserting foam along the inside arch, sew second bottom piece to remaining edge of strip. Turn right side out; insert foam in slipper and sew opening closed. Sew Felt and Fleece Flower to top of slipper.

BABY BLANKET

continued from page 8

Intersect and pin ribbon appliqués on blue fleece as shown on Placement Diagram. Work running stitches along center of rays to sew in place. Center and layer white fleece circle, then sun appliqué over ray intersection. Blanket stitch around sun. Pin cloud appliqués to blanket. For each cloud, leave an opening for stuffing and blanket stitch around cloud; stuff with fiberfill, then complete blanket stitches.

Placement Diagram

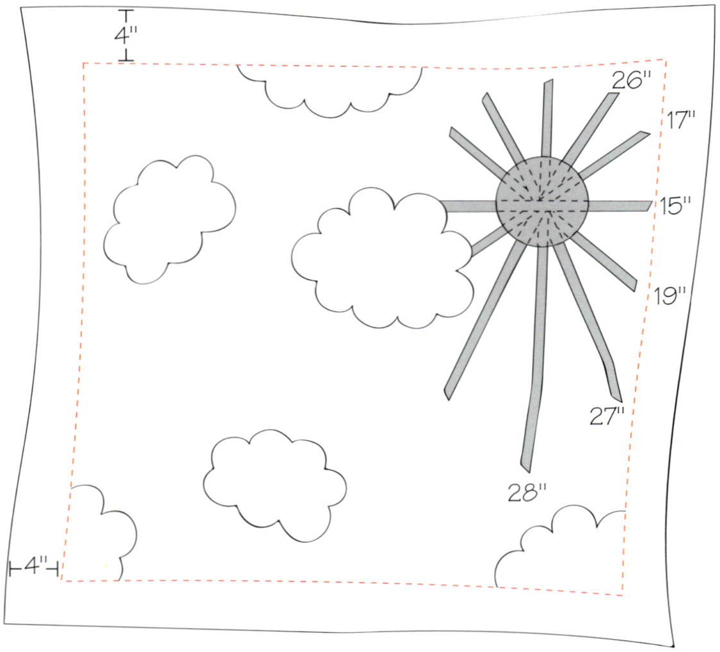

Matching wrong sides, pin fleece squares together. Cut 1/2"x3 1/2" fringe strips through top and bottom layers of fleece. Tie each top and bottom fringe strip together with a single wrap.

BABY GIRL JACKET AND CAP

continued from page 9

Blanket stitch along cuffs, edges of jacket and collar. Sew snap and rosette to jacket at neck.

Fig. 1

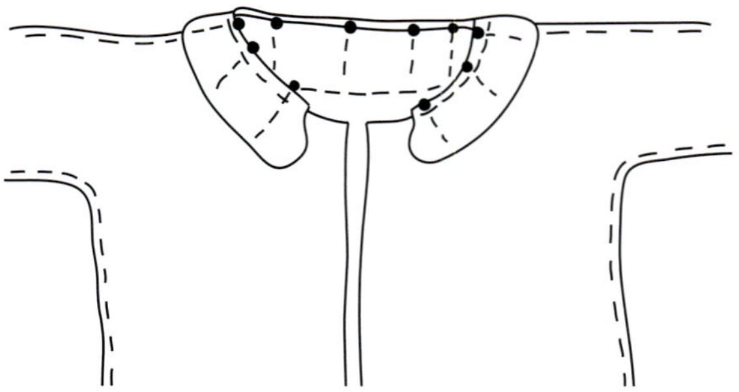

For cap, cut one 8"x16 1/2" rectangle from yellow fleece. For lining, cut one 8"x16 1/2" rectangle from white fleece. Sew ends of cap piece together; repeat for lining. Turn cap right side out. Matching seams and edges, insert cap in lining. Sew lining to cap along bottom edge; turn cap right side out. Sew a running stitch 2" from top of cap through both layers; trim lining close to stitching. Pull thread tight and wrap thread around gathers 3 times; knot to secure. Trim top of cap to desired length. Blanket stitch around bottom of cap. Turn cuff to right side and sew rosette to cuff.

LAMB

continued from page 10

Sew nose to face as shown (**Fig. 1**); clip curve of nose and press to right side. Repeat to sew face to head of one body piece. Sew eyes to face.

Fig. 1

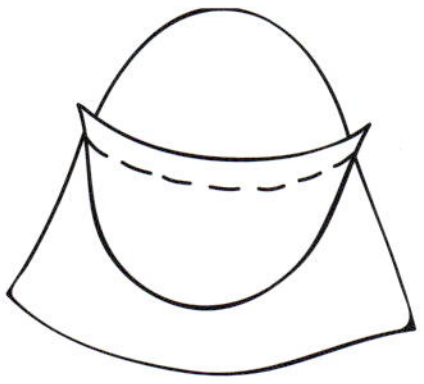

Matching edges, fold ears and tail in half with felt to inside; pin ears and tail to body as shown (**Fig. 2**). Leaving ends of legs and one side of lamb open for turning, sew body pieces together. Sew one foot shape to bottom of each leg. Turn lamb right side out. Stuff one leg with rice; sew across leg at body. Repeat for remaining legs. Stuff body with fiberfill; sew opening closed. Tie ribbon into a bow around neck; trim ends.

Fig. 2

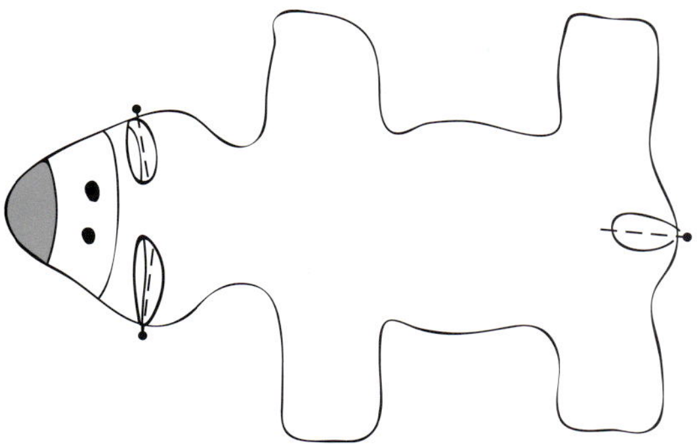

BABY BOY JACKET AND CAP

Photo, page 9; Basics, page 18; Patterns, page 28

- 5/8 yd blue textured fleece
- embroidery floss
- rotary cutter and cutting mat

Match right sides and raw edges and use a 1/4" seam allowance for all sewing unless noted. When cutting out pieces, make sure the fleece stretches across the pieces horizontally. Our finished cap has a 16" head opening; adjust the size of fleece rectangles as needed.

Enlarge jacket and cuff patterns 135% on photocopier. For jacket, used enlarged patterns to cut one jacket back, 2 (one in reverse) jacket fronts and 4 cuffs from fleece. Sew one cuff to end of each sleeve. Sew jacket fronts to jacket back along shoulder seams to dot. Sew side seams from bottom of jacket to end of cuffs; clip seams under arms. Turn jacket right side out. Fold cuffs into sleeves; blind stitch raw edges of cuffs in sleeves. Blanket stitch along cuffs and edges of jacket. Follow dashed line on pattern to fold and tack corners of collar to jacket.

For cap and lining, cut two 8"x16 1/2" rectangles from fleece. Sew ends of cap piece together; repeat for lining. Turn cap right side out. Matching seams and edges, insert cap in lining. Sew lining to cap along bottom edge; turn cap right side out. Sew a running stitch 2 1/2" from top of cap through both layers. Cut 1/2"x2" fringe strips along top edge through both layers. Pull thread tight. Wrap thread around gathers 3 times; knot to secure. Blanket stitch around bottom of cap; turn cuff to right side.

Basics

WORKING WITH FLEECE

Yardages are based on 60" wide fleece with an estimated "usable width" of 56" after trimming selvages. Fleece strips are cut selvage to selvage unless otherwise noted.

When sewing fleece seams, you may want to place a 2" wide strip of tear-away stabilizer between fleece and the feed dogs on your sewing machine. This will prevent stretching and help the fleece feed through the machine more easily. Sew seams, then remove stabilizer.

To prevent appliqué pieces from stretching, you may wish to trace lines onto tracing paper. Then turn tracing paper pattern over to reverse patterns, and trace onto dull side of freezer paper. Lightly iron freezer paper patterns, shiny side down, on wrong side of fleece. Cut out fleece pieces. Remove freezer paper patterns.

FELT AND FLEECE FLOWER

Patterns, page 21

Cut flower petals from felt and leaves from fleece scrap. Cut three 1/2" diameter felt circles. Placing a felt circle between each pair of petals, stack largest to smallest petal. Tuck leaf beneath largest petal. Sew button through all layers.

SIZING PATTERNS

To change the size of a pattern, divide desired height or width (whichever is largest) of pattern by present height or width of pattern. Multiply the result by 100%. Photocopy the pattern at this percentage.

> For example: You want your pattern to be 8" high but the pattern on the page is 6" high. So, 8÷6=1.33x100%=133%. You would copy the pattern at 133%.

EMBROIDERY STITCHES

Use 3 strands of embroidery floss unless otherwise noted. Follow the stitch diagrams to bring the needle up at odd numbers and down at even numbers.

Blanket Stitch

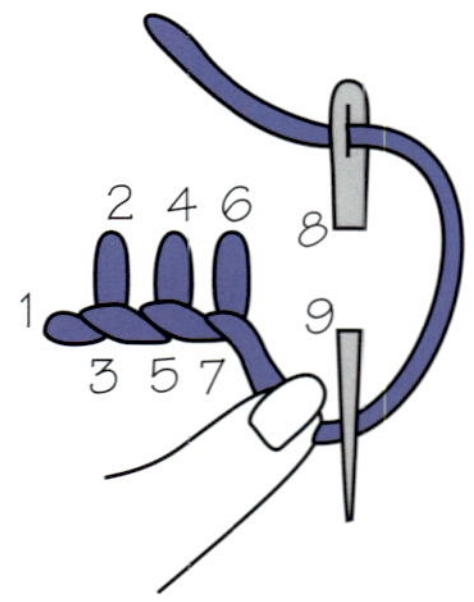

French Knot

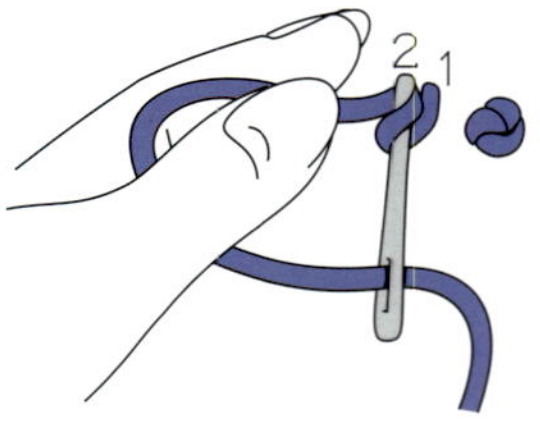

Running Stitch

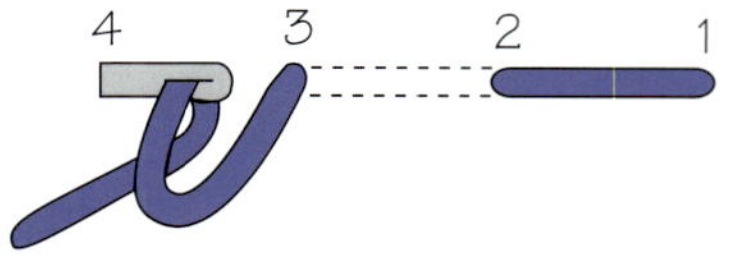

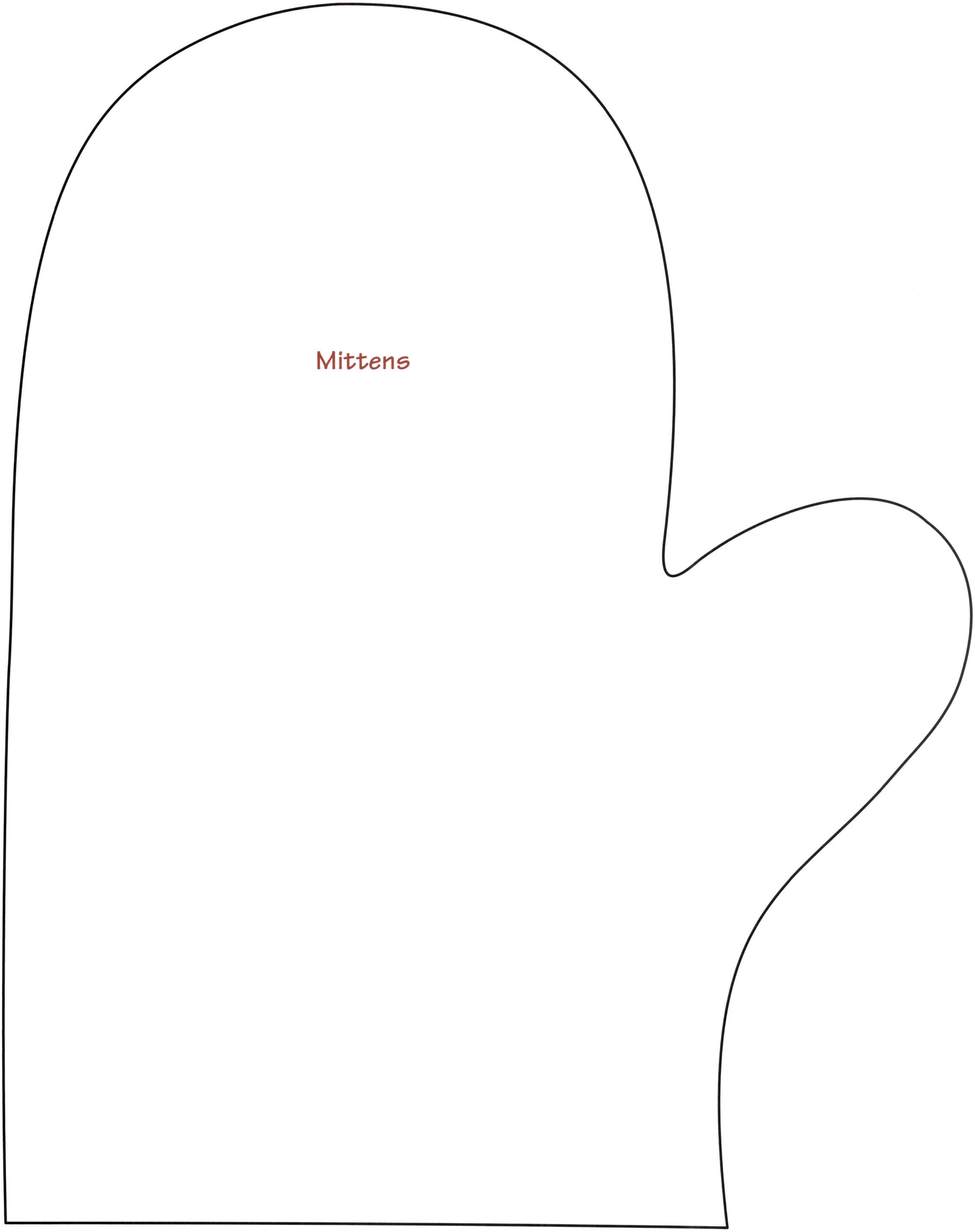
Mittens

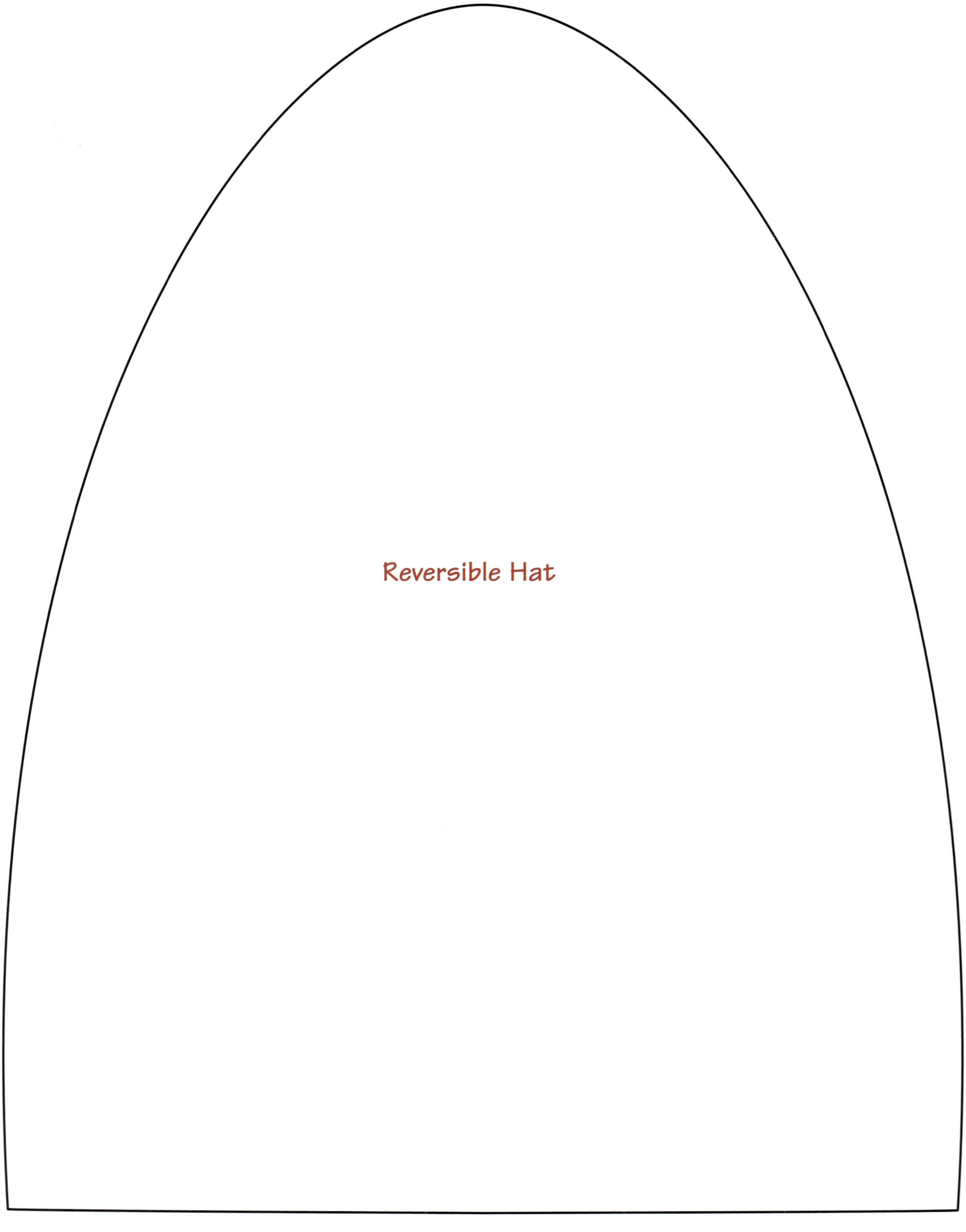
Reversible Hat

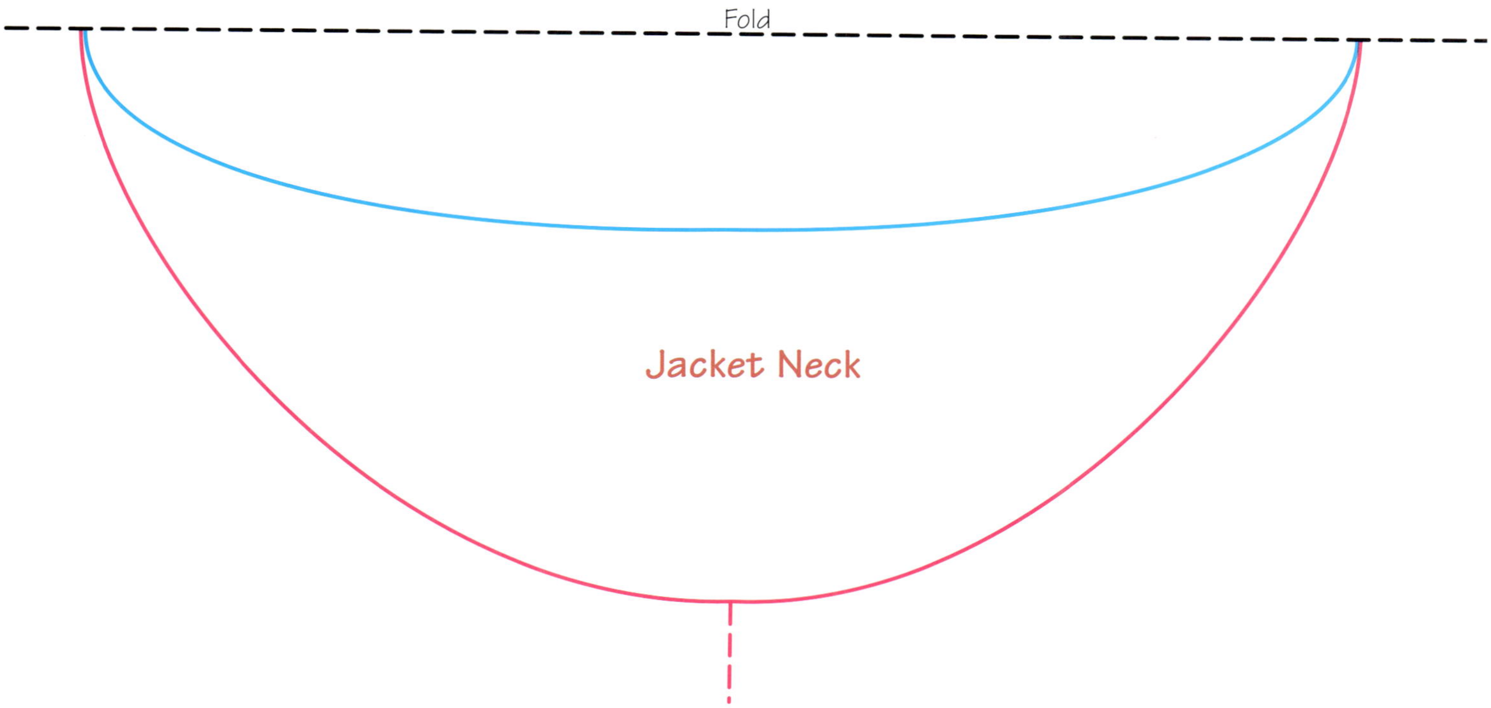
Fold
Jacket Neck

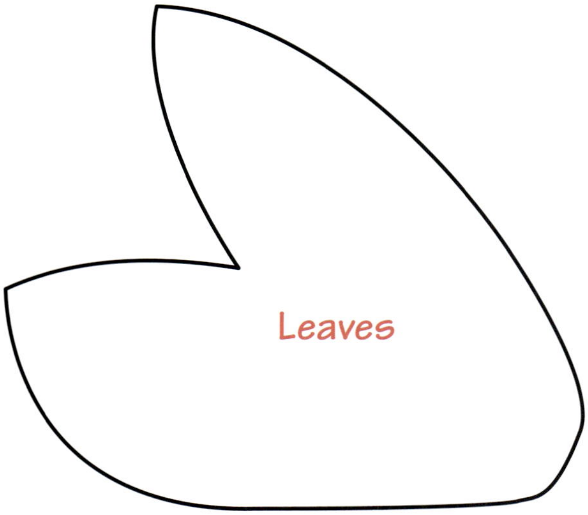
Leaves

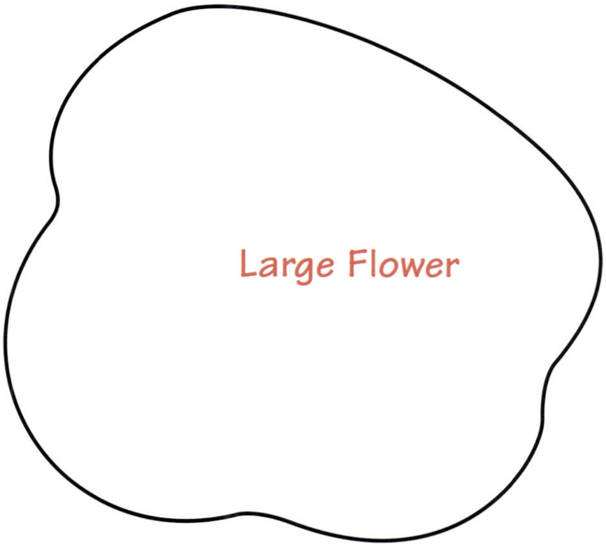
Large Flower

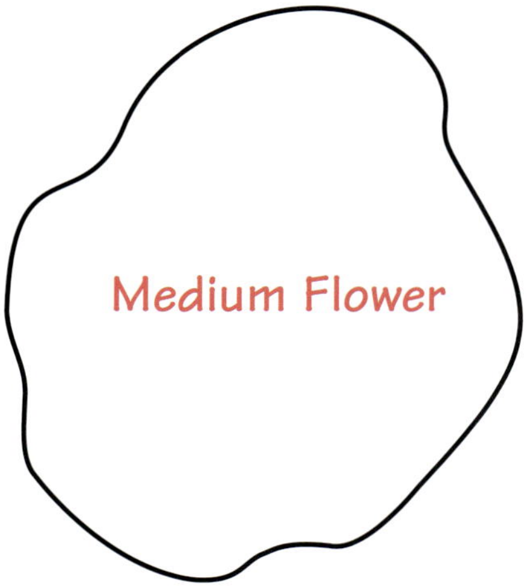
Medium Flower

Small Flower

Tiny Flower

NOP
QRST
UVW
XYZ

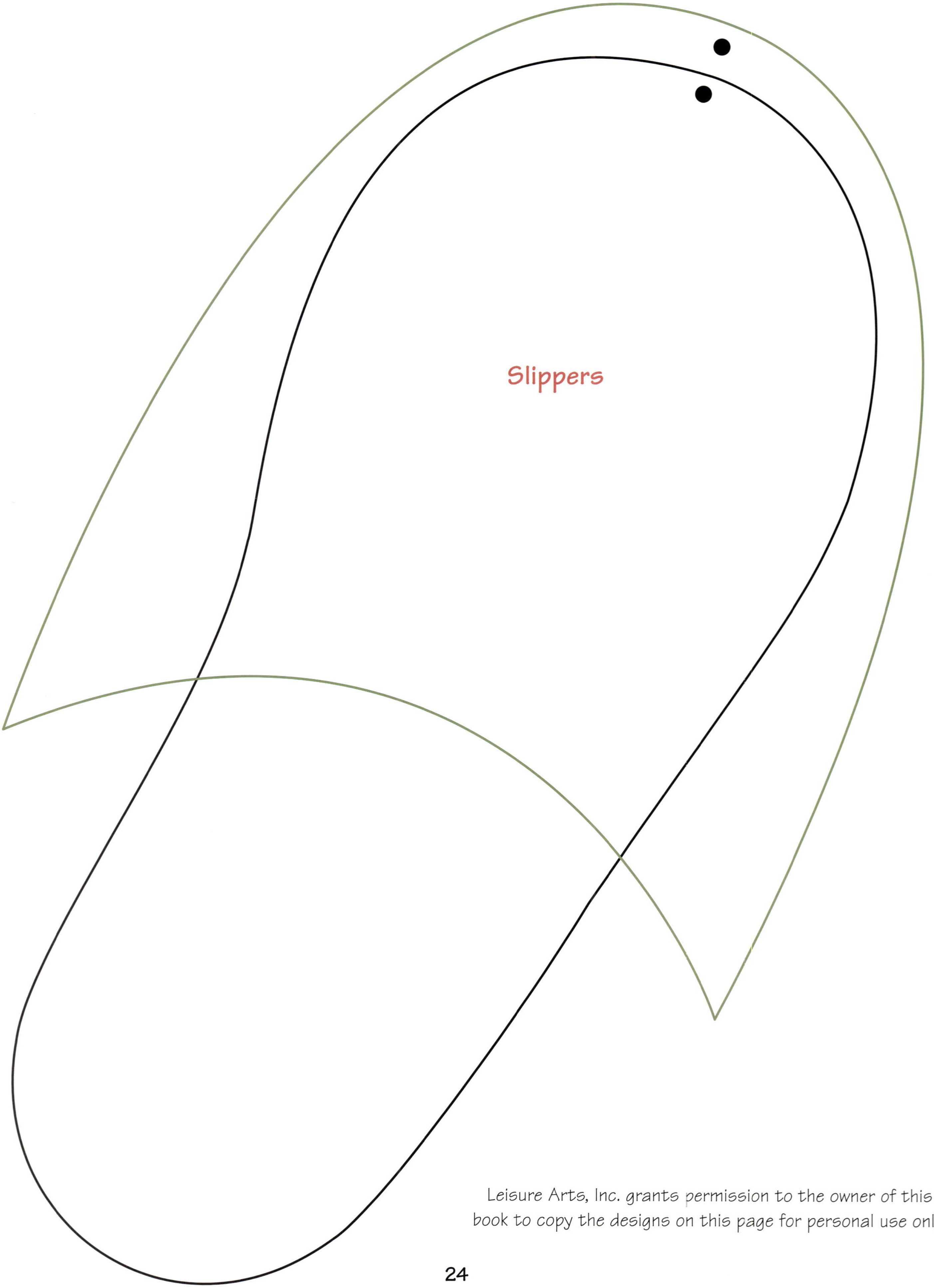
Slippers

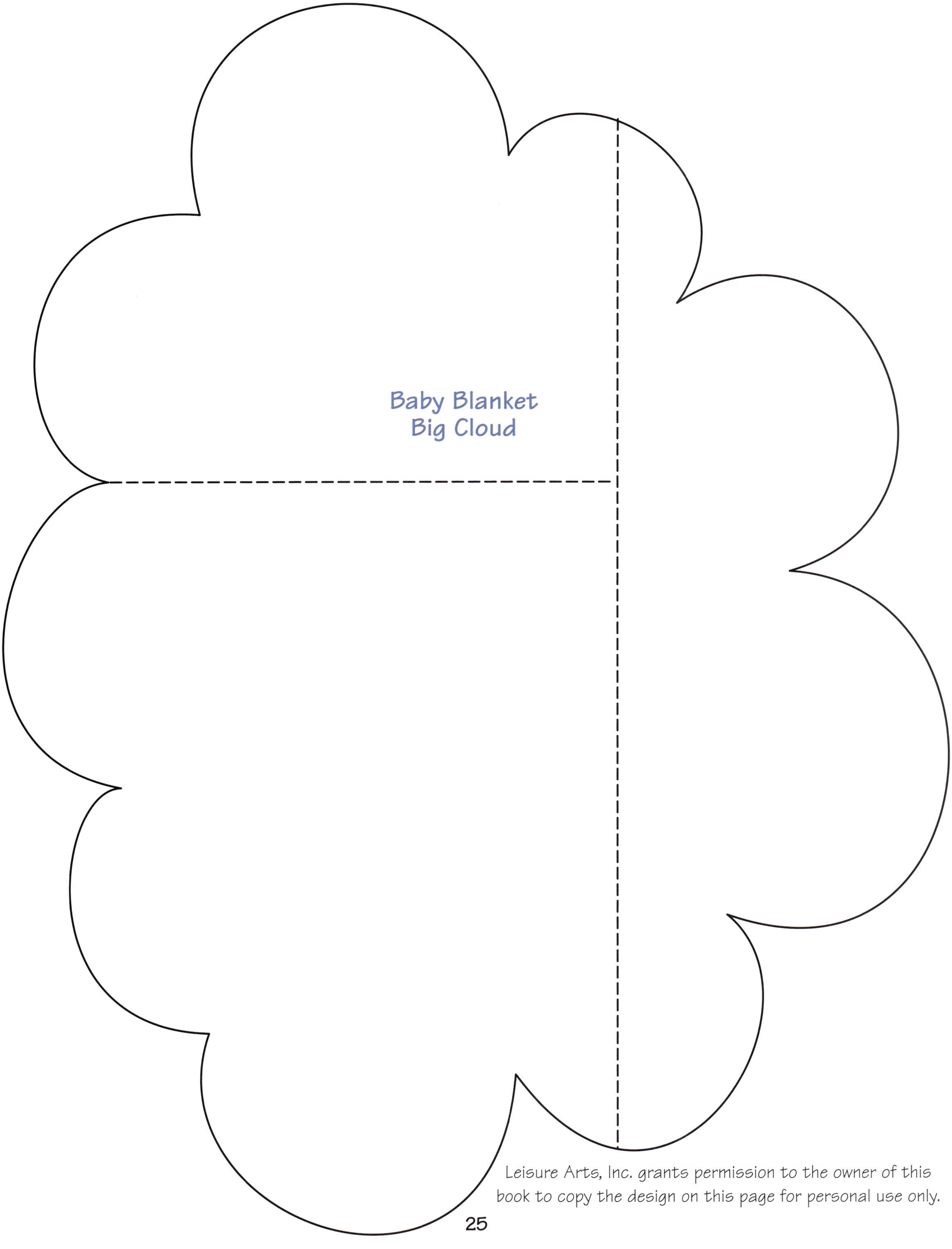
Baby Blanket
Big Cloud

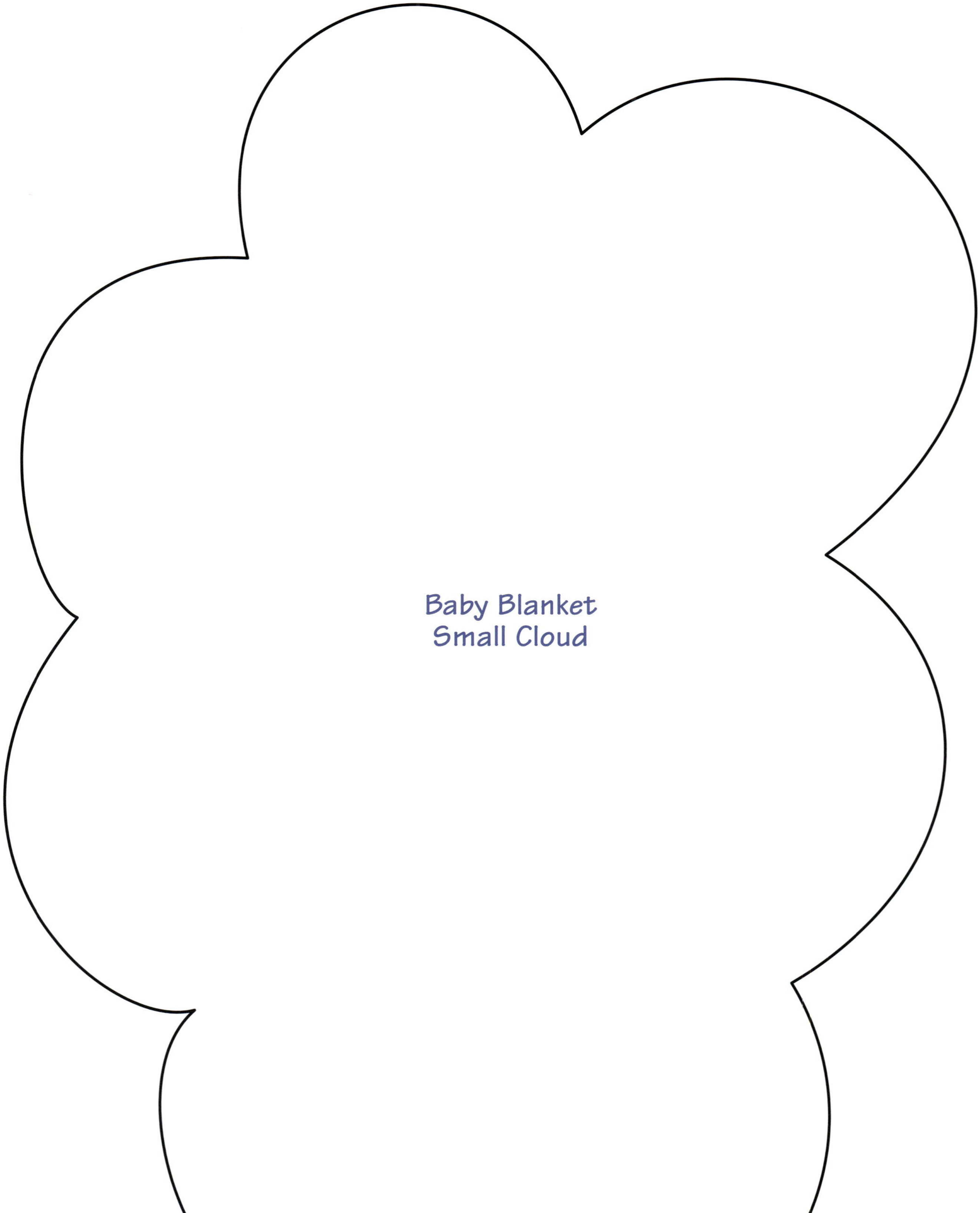
Baby Blanket
Small Cloud

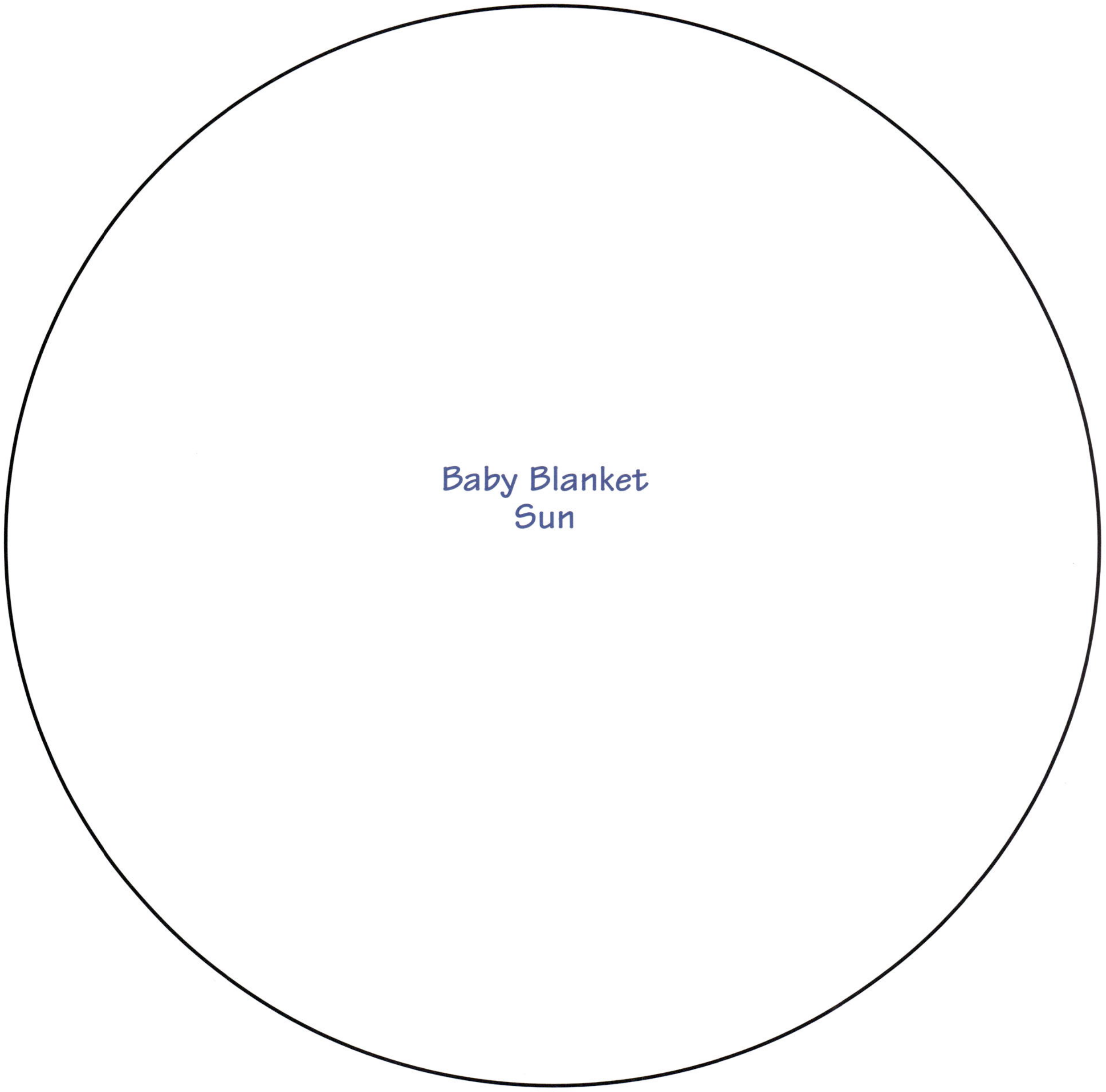
Baby Blanket
Sun

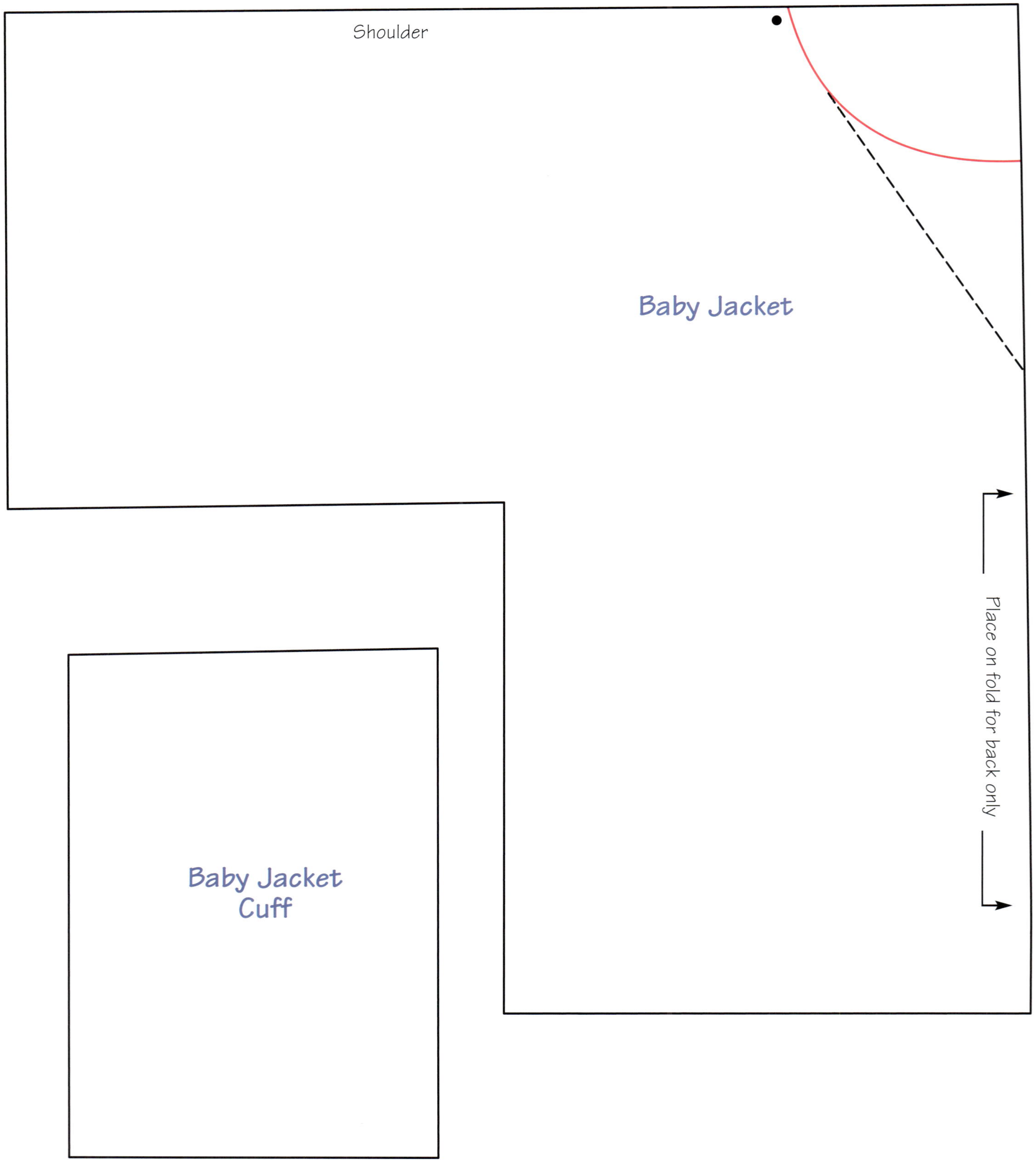
Shoulder
Baby Jacket
Place on fold for back only
Baby Jacket
Cuff

Boo-Boo Buddy

Boo-Boo Buddy

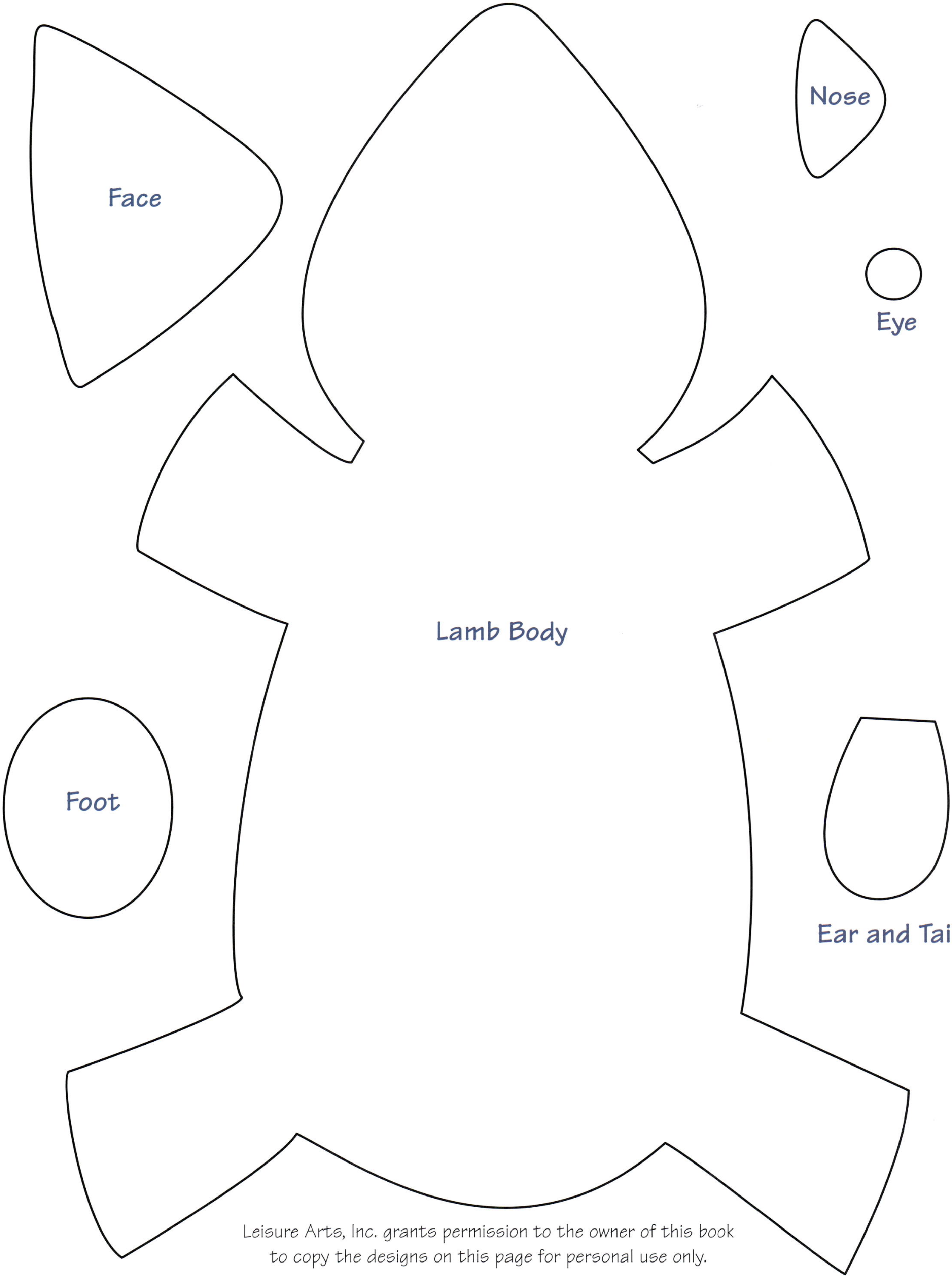
Face
Nose
Eye
Lamb Body
Foot
Ear and Tail

Metric Conversion Chart

Inches x 2.54 = centimeters (cm)	Yards x .9144 = meters (m)
Inches x 25.4 = millimeters (mm)	Yards x 91.44 = centimeters (cm)
Inches x .0254 = meters (m)	Centimeters x .3937 = inches (")
	Meters x 1.0936 = yards (yd)

Standard Equivalents

1/8"	3.2 mm	0.32 cm	1/8 yard	11.43 cm	0.11 m
1/4"	6.35 mm	0.635 cm	1/4 yard	22.86 cm	0.23 m
3/8"	9.5 mm	0.95 cm	3/8 yard	34.29 cm	0.34 m
1/2"	12.7 mm	1.27 cm	1/2 yard	45.72 cm	0.46 m
5/8"	15.9 mm	1.59 cm	5/8 yard	57.15 cm	0.57 m
3/4"	19.1 mm	1.91 cm	3/4 yard	68.58 cm	0.69 m
7/8"	22.2 mm	2.22 cm	7/8 yard	80 cm	0.8 m
1"	25.4 mm	2.54 cm	1 yard	91.44 cm	0.91 m

Embroidery floss provided courtesy of The DMC Corporation of South Kearny, New Jersey.

Nordic® fleece courtesy of David Textiles, Inc.

Baby Girl and Boy Jackets and Caps are adapted from designs by Bonnie Olaveson. Some instructions tested and photo models made by Diane Fischer, Jo Nortier and Kelly Reider.

Production Team: Designers — Tonya Bradford Bates, Polly Tullis Browning, Kim Kern, Anne Pulliam Stocks, Lori Wenger, and Becky Werle; Technical Writer — Laura Siar Holyfield; Editorial Writer — Steve Cooper; Graphic Artist — Amy Gerke; Photography Stylist — Sondra Daniel.

PRINTED WITH SOYINK

Made in U.S.A.